SILENT TEARS

THE LIFE OF A FORMER PASTOR'S WIFE

STEPHANIE C. SMITH

WestBow
PRESS
A DIVISION OF THOMAS NELSON

WestBow Press books may be ordered through booksellers or by contacting:

WestBow Press
A Division of Thomas Nelson
1663 Liberty Drive
Bloomington, IN 47403
www.westbowpress.com
1-(866) 928-1240

Because of the dynamic nature of the Internet, any web addresses or links contained in this book may have changed since publication and may no longer be valid. The views expressed in this work are solely those of the author and do not necessarily reflect the views of the publisher, and the publisher hereby disclaims any responsibility for them.

Any people depicted in stock imagery provided by Thinkstock are models, and such images are being used for illustrative purposes only.

Certain stock imagery © Thinkstock.

ISBN: 978-1-4497-1616-5 (sc)
ISBN: 978-1-4497-1615-8 (e)

Library of Congress Control Number: 2011927351

Printed in the United States of America

WestBow Press rev. date: 8/22/2011

DEDICATIONS

I dedicate this book to the memory of my grandfather Linwood Morris, Sr. and grandmother Fannie E. Morris for the solid foundation you gave me as a child and to the memory of my cousin Frank B. Slater. You are my brother and I miss you dearly. To my mother for the guidance, support and encouragement she has always given me throughout my life. To my children because you are the love of my life and my biggest cheerleaders, and to the ones that God turned around what you meant for evil in my life and He used it for my good. If it were not for you I would not have anything to write about. I would not be able to encourage others to use what they consider negative and make it a positive. You too can over come! Be Blessed!

INTRODUCTION

Do you believe things that happen to us in our childhood affects us as adults? I, for one, do believe that events in our childhood affect us as adults. They can affect us in a positive or negative way but I believe it is up to us to determine the outcome. It is up to us to forgive so we can heal and not give the person or people that hurt us the power to control our lives. Whether you realize it or not, you give power to the person or people that hurt you power by holding on to the hurt.

They may never ask you for forgiveness and live their lives as if nothing ever happened. That is ok, move on with your dreams, aspirations, and desires you have for your life. If writing a book is your form of healing, then do that. Share your story, testimony, or deliverance with others. Let them know if God can do it for you he can do it for them. You just have to be willing to move pass the hurt and unforgiveness and then the healing process will begin. You never know who you will touch through your story and change their life.

For years, I was ashamed of my past. I did not want anyone to know about my life. I had to seek God for deliverance. I came to the understanding that God was there with me and my children through it all. I have thought about a way I could share my story because I know there was someone else out there that may have experienced the same situation or a similar situation. They may feel there is no light at the end of the tunnel. They may feel God has forsaken them. They may feel as though they are the only ones that have even gone through what they are experiencing or have experienced and there is no hope. They may be ashamed of their testimony. They don't want to be judged.

God finally released me to write this book. I am not ashamed of my past anymore. I know God had a plan. I always wondered what my purpose was. Now I know. It is to share my story with the world so that others can be delivered from religious bondage, people, abuse, control. Maybe even another pastor's wife may need to read my book and get strength to be all God has called her to be. My life now is literally an open book.

CHAPTER I

My grandmother and grandfather played an intricate part in the early stages of my life. I would visit them often when I was young. I enjoyed visiting them because I was an only child and I had a lot of first cousins to play with when I would come to visit them. I was especially close to my grandfather. Maybe that was because my father was not a stable part of my life.

I can remember July 4, 1972 as if it was just yesterday. I was visiting my grandparents for the summer. I was at my aunt and uncle's home outside playing with fireworks with my cousins. My grandfather came to pick me up but I was not ready to leave. My aunt talked him into letting me stay, he agreed. It seemed like only a few minutes had passed when I saw my aunt run outside very upset and crying. My cousins and I were wondering what was going on. Then my aunt said that my granddaddy had just been in a serious car accident. My grandmother was able to make it to the hospital before he passed away.

I was 6 years old at the time so I really was not clear about what had happened. All I knew was that my granddaddy was not gonna be around anymore. As I got older I realized that if I had been in the car I could have lost my life also. God had a plan for my life.

My mother was living in another state at the time. After the death of my granddaddy my mom and I moved in with my grandmother. My mother was a single parent at the time and she made sure I never wanted or needed anything. My grandmother had my mom's back as well. She always made sure breakfast and dinner was done when we got home from school. I had the best of both worlds, my grandma and my mommy. I was not close to my father because he was not in my life at the time. My grandmother and mommy kept me grounded. They raised me based on spiritual values and I am grateful for that.

As a child we tend to subconsciously remember things that happened to us in our childhood and build a defense mechanism as an adult as an attempt to make sure it does not happen to us again. My mom made sure I had a complete childhood. I performed well in school, was a cheerleader, participated in the concert and marching band and I was active in church. I never felt as though I was missing anything in my life. I just wanted to make sure I made my mother proud of me. I never wanted to disappoint her.

After high school I attended college. I became pregnant my sophomore year and had to withdraw from college for a year. I always had a drive to overcome obstacles which are just temporary set backs. I wanted to be home with my daughter for the first year of her life so I sat out for 1987. My baby was born in 1986. I was supposed to graduate from college in 1988. I was determined to finish 1 year after my original graduation date and I knew in order to do that I had to work hard. I attended summer school in the summer of 1987 and 1988 which allowed me to graduate in May 1989. I worked a part-time job and I was a single mother.

My mother and grandmother had my daughter while I was in college. I would go home every other weekend to be with her. Getting pregnant in college could have caused me to just drop out but it motivated me even more to obtain my degree.

You see, you can do whatever you put your mind to. You have to want it. I have always been a private person and would only share what I wanted you to know. I did not want people to see me any differently. I had to wait until the time was right to share my story. I know there are other women out there that may feel trapped by the choices they have made in life. I am here to tell you, today you can change your mind set. You can begin to accomplish those goals you have set for yourself.

Chapter II

While in college I worked part-time for a call center. While I was there I met a young man there. He also had a daughter. He was a nice guy, a nice dresser, and he made me laugh. Honestly, he was not my type at first but then we began to spend time together and as I got to know him he grew on me. We began to date and he proposed to me. After I graduated we were married the same year. I was 23 years old. We had a beautiful wedding. It was the type of wedding I dreamed about. Because of my spiritual beliefs and values I believed we would be married forever. There was just one thing that stood out to me. He cried during the entire ceremony.

We had our arguments and fights in the beginning but nothing major that would prepare me for what was about to happen. He gave me a birthday party in 1990. Our friends and some family members attended the party. I noticed a woman that I did not know personally. She had been invited by him. The party was really nice. We had so much fun.

To my surprise about a week or so after my party my husband moved out. I had no idea where he was or why he did that to me and our daughters. I was a mess. My job started to suffer and my supervisor confronted me about my performance. I was not eating, I cried all the time. I realized I had to gather enough strength to care for my daughter because she needed me. I could not figure out what had happened. Why did he abandon me? What did I do wrong?

About 2 weeks after he moved out I was going into my house and my neighbor who used to ride to work with him had approached me. The neighbor said he knew where my husband was. He told me my husband had moved in with a woman he worked with. He told me where they were living and it was only about 5 minutes from where we lived. Unbelievable right? Guess what else, to top it off it was that strange woman that was at my party that I did not know.

I became very angry! How dare he do this to me? I even felt as though I lowered my standards to even marry him and now he's going to do something like this to me. Well, I used my detective skills and found out the exact apartment. I saw his car parked out front, went home and got ALL his belongings and put it on top of his car.

That was it, I was a faithful dedicated wife and he goes and commits adultery? I was not excepting that. The marriage was over. A couple of years later, I was able to become his friend and he confided in me. He apologized for what he had done to me in our marriage and told me he was gay. Yes, he said he was gay. He said he knew he had those feelings when he married me. I asked if he had been with other men before and or during our marriage and he told me he had not. He said he had been fighting those feelings for years and that he moved in with that woman because he was trying give me a reason to end our marriage. When I thought back I asked if that was why he was crying during the ceremony because he was confused and he said yes.

Yes, I was angry and relieved at the same time. I was angry because I believed in "till death do us part" and he should have dealt with these issues before he asked me to marry him. I had a peace because I knew it was nothing I had done. He had these feelings long before he met me.

By this time in my life my mother and father had begun to work on their marriage. I had gotten past any childhood issues I had with my father and was able to develop a friendship with him. In 1994 I was 26 years old. Guess I needed to find myself. I decided I wanted to go in the military. I told my dad about it so he took me to take the test. We did not tell my mom because we knew she would have reservations about my decision. My score was high enough for me to enter the Army as an E-4 since I already had a college degree.

I joined the United States Army Reserve. I was given a date for basic training and the location. At this point I knew I had to tell my mother because this was real and was going to happen. Needless to say she was not thrilled about my decision but she was supportive and so was my dad. While I was in basic training I was the Platoon Leader and it was my responsibility to supervise 54 women. Talk about stressful. I enjoyed every minute of it. This process allowed me to tap into my strengths and I am a better woman because of that experience.

My mother and father attended my Basic Training and Advanced Individual Training graduation ceremony. I received honors for my leadership and performance in school. My parents were very proud of me. I returned to my hometown. I had no idea of what my plans would be as far as employment. I just knew I had to report for my reserve duty once a month.

I remembered my best friend worked for the Employment Commission in our area so I contacted her. She was able to set me up for an interview with a company that had a security contract with NASA. I interviewed and was offered the job as the Security Clerk. This would be the beginning of my "Silent Tears".

CHAPTER III

I enjoyed my job and working with my co-workers. I had an extremely long commute but I liked my job, so I was able to deal with the commute. After a few months there I began to receive a dozen roses from an admirer for an entire week. I did not have the slightest idea who it could have been. Well, after about 2 weeks that person finally came forth. He was the Sergeant in my department. We worked closely together but I never suspected him because I never looked at him as anymore than just a co-worker.

I did not want to hurt his feelings but I let him know I was not interested in him. He was persistent and continued to ask me to go to dinner. I finally figured "well one date won't hurt". So I accepted his invitation to dinner. The date turned into dating. It was good at first then I started to notice he was becoming controlling at work. He would get upset if men would look at me. He would not want me to assist any men at all which made it difficult for me to do my job because I worked with mostly men and the visitors to the base were men.

Yes, I chose to ignore the signs. Guess it seemed like he was giving me his undivided attention, which he was but it was not healthy attention. As time went on, I continued to ignore all of the obvious signs of control. The relationship became serious and we decided to move in together. I took my daughter and we started a new life living with this man against my better judgment. If I could change the past I would in the snap of a finger.

He talked me into quitting my job which I enjoyed because I loved my independence. Each time I was giving him more and more control of me and who I was but I did not realize it at the time. I allowed him to start dictating to my daughter as far as her behavior. She was not a bad child at all. She was an average child and very smart. If there was a situation in school concerning her instead of me taking care of it he would want to handle the situation.

Now the abuse begins. I would express to him my concerns regarding allowing me to be the parent I should be to my daughter and that I did not always agree with how he chose to handle certain situations and we would argue about that. Well, he hit me and we began to fight. After the altercation I packed my things and my daughter's things and told him I was leaving. He begged me to stay and he cried and yes, I stayed. This may sound crazy but I felt sorry for him and believed he really loved me and he would never do it again. Did it continue to happen? YES. We would argue and fight about how irrational he was when it came to my daughter and me being allowed to have a life and think for myself. He just had to control everything and everybody. I would threatened to leave all the time but he would change my mind because I felt he needed me.

I received a call from my dad who said my grandmother had passed. He wanted to attend the service with me, guess he thought I was not gonna come back. I shouldn't have.

I remember his sister had come home to visit and she bought her male friend with her. After our visit had come to an end and we were about to say our good-byes, her friend kissed me on my cheek. Oh my goodness! What did he do that for? When we got in the car we argued all the way home about that. He felt he should not have done that and I should not have allowed that to happen. I asked why he didn't confront the man about it and not me. He hit me so hard in my right ear that all I heard was ringing. I prayed I would not lose my hearing in that ear.

It happened, I became pregnant. I already had one child before I was married and I did not want that to happen again. I felt I had to be responsible and stay with him. I am an educated woman. I can't have 2 children and not be married.

He kept my daughter and me sheltered from my family. I had begun to allow him to give me permission for everything. If I wanted to talk to my mother I would have to call her when he wasn't there. My mother had an idea of what I was going through with him but she never got involved. I believed she felt this was a choice I had to make and I know she prayed that I made the right decision.

I remember there was this time she wanted me and my daughter to go to visit my aunt, her sister, in Philadelphia. I was about 5 months pregnant. I told him about it and he had a fit. He did not want us to go.

His mother even got involved in it and told him he was not being rational, she explained this was my mother and I was grown and did not have to ask his permission for anything. I decided to go and he was very angry. I did not care. That was the most enjoyable time I had in my life in a very long time.

He did allow someone from the outside to come into our inner circle and that was his sister and her friend. They would come to visit us and we would play spades. We were not saved at the time. They were Christians and would always talk about God and the church they belonged to. Someone may feel or think they were hypocrites because they would play cards with us. Well, we did not gamble and they had to meet us at our level so that they could minister to us.

We continued to play spades with them for about a year. They would always invite us to visit their church. I was desperate; I wanted a change in my life and a change in the relationship that I had with this man because I was miserable. I hated how he treated me and my daughter. I felt that if we would go to church, God would change him and the control would stop, the fighting would stop, and he would become a loving father to our unborn child.

I finally convinced him that we should go to church with his sister. The service was awesome. I felt God tugging at my heart. Visitors were asked to stand, and we obeyed and he introduced me and my daughter to the congregation. While he was speaking he began crying saying how he wanted to change his life and that he was glad he came to church that day. During alter call, the congregation stood and I remember the pastor saying to him "Brother you want a change for you and your family, then let's start today with you and your family coming to the altar for prayer". That day we both gave our lives to Christ and joined the church.

CHAPTER IV

So here we are. I'm starting to show, we are going to church, living together and not married. We began to memorize scriptures and quiz each other. We were starting to grow together spiritually, now he started to use the scripture to control me. Oh my goodness. I can't win for losing. We would be riding in the car and he would accuse me of looking at other men in their cars. It was crazy. I am carrying this man's child, still living with him, not married, in the church, and wondering if I even want to be with him. Should I just leave and have two children by 2 different men or stay and be miserable? I had so much of my life to share, my experiences but he did not want me to talk about them. Guess my life was supposed to have started when I met him.

There was a Good Friday service at our church and he was one of the speakers for the program. After everyone on the program had spoken he comes back up to the podium. I hear him say I need to get my life completely in order with God and do the right thing for my family. Then he looks at me and says in front of the entire church, Stephanie, will you marry me? I was speechless. My mind was racing, I was thinking "he acts one way at home and another way at church; well maybe if we get married he will change because he asked me in church in front of everyone, what if he doesn't change? *Lord, I am miserable; I don't want to be his wife. Is this a set-up to get me to except his proposal because he has asked me in front of the entire church? I am sitting here pregnant living with this man and we are in the church. Everyone is waiting for a response. If I don't accept what will the church think of me? They don't understand what I go through at home with this man. All they see is a smile always on my face. They don't know the silent tears I have on the inside. Oh God help me! What should I do? I want*

11

to leave him. With his mouth he says one thing and with his actions I am his property, not an equal. But God, I know you can change him. Will this be a union ordained by God?

I opened my mouth and the word "yes" came out. Everyone in the church applauded, stood up, came over and gave me hugs. They were so happy. All they saw and knew was the fact that we were doing the right thing in the sight of God.

We are engaged now and I couldn't even greet the brothers in the church with a hug or even make eye contact without him accusing me of flirting with them. Everywhere I went he had to go. I couldn't even be friends with or even visit the ladies in the church. Guess he did not want me getting too close to anyone because I may disclose what goes on behind closed doors. Did anyone know my pain? Of course not, I was always smiling, always happy.

It was December, I am 8 months pregnant and about to walk down the aisle at this point in my life. Now that God was in my life, the feelings I had for my father when I was growing up have become those of a little girl who was to be "daddy's little girl". He was going to give me away. It is the day of the wedding and I am preparing for the ceremony. This is supposed to be my special day. I get a call from my soon to be husband who tells me not to put on too much make-up and to make sure I don't get fake nails. I know crazy right? You got to be kidding me! Lord, is this yet another sign? The day has arrived and I can't back out now. Now, it's starting to snow, is this another sign?

I have arrived to the church. I am preparing to walk down the aisle with my father. I hug my daddy and start crying uncontrollably. I had to get my make-up redone. Was I crying because I felt on the inside that I was making a BIG mistake? My daddy reassured me that everything was ok and that he loved me so we proceeded down the aisle. As I am standing at the altar I felt numb. There was no feeling of excitement at all. I felt as though this was an obligation. I was going to be married before my baby is born. This is his first child so he was excited about that. I knew in my heart that I was doing the wrong thing for what I felt was the right reasons. I felt I had completely lost my identity to this man. I knew my life was going to change forever.

CHAPTER V

In January I gave birth to a healthy baby girl. Our church was not located in the state in which we resided so we decided to move closer to the church. We bought a house and were excited about the move. I prayed this would be a new lease on life for us. I started to see the growth in him spiritually. God was using him for his glory; however, he did not treat his family the way that would be expected of a Christian man. I wanted to be a faithful wife so I trusted God to strengthen our marriage and give him the revelation he needed to be that husband and father God called him to be.

One time he wanted to discipline our oldest daughter (his step daughter) over something small, I did not agree with it so we argued about it. I remember he slapped me then placed his hands around my throat and started choking me. The only way I stopped him from choking me was to punch him as hard as I could upside his head. I am sure the kids heard the commotion. To make sure he did not try anything once I got away from him, I picked up the phone and told him I would call 9-1-1 and have him locked up. He was stalled by that and became apologetic.

Apparently our pastor saw the anointing in his life. He was being asked to speak when there were special services. I must say, God used him to bring forth the word. God would give him awesome revelation on the word and use him mightily.

There was a church in the area that was in need of a pastor. Representatives from the church came to talk to our pastor about the need to find an Interim pastor. Our pastor recommended my husband. There were a lot of more seasoned ministers in our church and our pastor recommended him. He had only been a minister for about 3-6 months.

I always said I never wanted to be a pastor's wife. I suppose God had a different plan for my life. I could not see it then but years later I see things more clearly. I will explain later.

The church offered him the position as Interim pastor and he accepted so now the children and I had to start attending this new church where we did not know anyone. I had so much anxiety. Would they accept us? Would they be friendly? Were we walking into something we had no idea about? Why did they need another pastor? Was there drama that we were going to become a part of? Was there someone else they were looking at as becoming the pastor? I was so nervous. We were about to leave the church family that embraced us and welcomed us with welcome arms.

It was the first Sunday at the church. My husband was now the Interim pastor and I was the first lady. What did that mean exactly? Am I supposed to act a certain way? Am I not supposed to be myself? Am I supposed to always be happy even when I am crying on the inside? Am I supposed to be submissive to my husband even when I did not agree with him? Am I supposed to keep my opinions to myself and believe that whatever he says goes?

We were welcomed with open arms; however, I could sense the tension. There were some members who were comfortable with him as Interim pastor and others who may not have been as comfortable with the idea but we were still shown love. There was another person who was a member of the church that was also being considered to be the pastor. Apparently they had already served as Interim pastor so now after my husband's duty as Interim pastor the congregation would then vote. Even though I could sense the tension I was always shown love and respected. That was all that mattered.

How was my home life now since my husband was the Interim pastor? Had things made a change for the better? No, things were worse. He had become more controlling. He would use the bible to "keep me in my place". I could not even go to the store by myself. He felt the need to chauffer me everywhere. We would argue or fight on a Saturday night before he had to preach on Sunday. Yes, I would go to bed angry with him. He would act like nothing happened and would not ask me to forgive him. We would ride in the same car to church. I would be mad as I don't know what! He would have just hit me on Saturday, write his sermon for Sunday, and then drive to church to preach Sunday morning. Unbelievable!

Before he would preach he would have the ministers and I join him in his office to pray with him before he would preach. I would be standing there thinking, "you are such a hypocrite, you just put your hands on me last night and did not ask me to forgive you, and now you have the nerve to pray to God for his anointing so you can preach"! After he finished praying everyone would leave out the office and he would ask me to stay. He would then say he was sorry. I would just look at him and say ok then walk out of the office.

I was a supportive wife during his position as acting pastor. I would lay his clothes out for him and cook. He would not have to lift a finger. Sometimes to him it would feel like those that did not want him to become the pastor would be fighting him all the way. I would encourage him even though my life at home was a nightmare. I would reassure him that God had a calling on his life and that God was faithful and had not bought him this far to leave him. There were times as with any marriage where it was good and I was ok with the marriage but then when he would not act like a man of God and lash out at me and my oldest child, I began to think he was not stable mentally.

I wanted to leave so many times, but I felt obligated to stay there especially now that he was a pastor. I could not understand it. I hated being married to him but I held the faith that it would get better because God honors marriage and I had already been married before so I have to make it work. The reality is, God gives us a will. The fact that I married him does not mean that it was the will or plan God had for me. However, I chose to marry this man and I was gonna try to hang in there with the help of God.

Chapter VI

The time had come for the congregation to vote for the next pastor of their church. I believed the selection process was done decently and in order. Nerves were on edge as the selection could have gone either way. What if I told the congregation about how miserable I am as his wife? How he is abusive and that the children were afraid of him. Would that make a difference in who they would choose to be the pastor of the church? Should I let them know that he is one way at home and another at church? Is that my responsibility? Who am I to say God has not called this man to lead his people. Maybe he just needs deliverance.

The votes were in and he was selected to be the pastor. I was happy for him. Maybe as the pastor he will be the man he is supposed to be at home. Or is it still wishful thinking? He was installed as the pastor. We were now the "first family". We have two children I am expecting our third child, I am a stay at home mother and he was the pastor and he worked two jobs.

He decided to go to Bible College to get his Associate degree in ministry. The classes were held on Monday nights. He did not like to order out. My oldest daughter and I looked forward to Monday nights. We would order pizza. We would hide the box in the dumpster so he would not know we had ordered out. We often talk about that now.

His insecurities seemed to have gotten worse. He wanted me to start dressing a certain way. I had to wear my shirt on the outside of my pants and my pants had to be baggy not form fitting at all. He justified this by saying he did not want other men looking at me. He did not want me wearing make-up of any kind and I could not get my nails done. If I went to get my hair done which was not often, he had to tell the stylist how he wanted it styled. I felt like a child. It was very embarrassing. I did not have a voice and if I voiced my opinion we would end up in a fight.

I spoke to my mother on this particular day. She informed me that my father had been diagnosed with cancer. She said the doctor had put him on medication and they were going to try that before chemo or radiation treatment. I knew my mother needed my support and I wanted to be there for her and my father. We only had one car. He acted as if he could not take me to spend time with my parents and he did not want them to come get me. He had cut me off from my entire family. I could only imagine what my family thought and how they felt. I was not allowed to be with my parents while they were going through this devastating time in their lives. If only they knew the torment I was going through in my home. I felt brain washed, hopeless, and helpless. Can they understand he had broken me down to the point that he made me only dependent on him. I'm sorry I have no more fight left. I was just existing, going through the motions, smiling on the outside while crying on the inside. I wanted someone, anyone to help me. I was in pain. I was tired of putting up this façade.

My father had taken a turn for the worse. My aunt called us and my husband answered the phone as usual. She spoke with him. She pleaded with him to bring me to see my father as he had gotten worse. This remains so vivid in my mind. He told her that he would. After he finished the conversation with my aunt and hung up the phone, he looked at me and told me what my aunt had said to him, then he said, "Why rush now, we can't do anything all we can do is pray". I told him he was heartless and if that had been someone in his family he would have been at his family's side. I was so bitter about this for years. I had to release it because I started to hate him and I knew that this was not the Godly thing to do.

We did not go that evening to see my father but we did go the next day. I did not want my husband anywhere near me but of course he watched me like a hawk. Guess he wanted to make sure I did not disclose his dirty little secrets of abuse and control. I could tell my daddy was not going to be with us much longer. He wasn't very responsive. I felt so guilty that I had not been there for him and my mother, that I had allowed this man to control every aspect of my life. I could not see things clearly then. I was concerned about how it would look to the church if I left him. After all he was a pastor and I was the first lady of the church. I always put his feelings before my own. I was so selfless and he was so selfish.

The next day I got the call that my father had passed. I thank God for allowing me to see him and spend a few moments with him before he took him home. God is so awesome and even though I was going through with my marriage and was being controlled by this person God showed me he was with me by allowing me and my daddy to have a moment before he left this earth.

My husband, daughters, and I attended the funeral. While we were at my mother's house getting ready before the service he made sure he kept us close. He would not even allow the girls to just hang out around their Nana's house. They had to be up under us. Everyone noticed that. I felt so uncomfortable and he made sure he wore his clergy collar.

We were sitting in the kitchen and my heart dropped. My ex-husband and dear friend of mine walked in the kitchen. We all had small talk and I was praying my ex-husband did not say anything that would have my husband figure out he was my ex-husband because I knew I would hear it and it would not be pretty. I knew that would be a serious issue because he was extremely insecure. He never figured it out. We left for the church and he had no clue who he was. He just thought he was an old family friend.

After the service everyone returned to the house. Our family and friends were there paying their respect. Of course we could not take part. He had all of us lay down for a nap upstairs. Yes, the whole family had to take a nap. This was a method he used to make sure we did not communicate with anyone. My family and I laugh about it now but at that time we did not see the humor because this man was obviously sick. When I think abut how I allowed myself to be treated in that manner and made to function like a robot I thank God he helped me snap out of it. I realize this, we all can say "if it were me I would or would not have….." that is easy to say unless you live it. Remember this, if not for the grace of God…..

CHAPTER VII

I now see the characteristics of an abuser. To cause you to be dependent on them by keeping you secluded from your loved ones and not allow you to have friends. To break you down to nothing and then make you the way they want you to be.

He was being called to preach at different churches and it started to go to his head. He was comfortable with being a pastor acting one way at church and having a horrible life at home. He felt as long as he asked God to forgive him he was ok. He finally allowed me to get a job outside of the house. I was so happy. The job was about a 45 min commute one way. Yes, he took me to work and picked me up everyday.

The job I had required me to be on the phone so I had a direct line to my desk. He would call me on my job everyday at least 3 times a day and he did not want anything. The call was long distance so our phone bill was ridiculously high. That was it! I had enough! I started making preparation to pack up the kids and leave him. I was sick of it all! I could not have any friends. I could not even go out shopping or dinner with the women of the church. I was angry, I did not care how it made him look anymore. I was going to leave him.

There was a young lady that I met that lived near us that worked at the same company where I worked. I convinced him to let me ride to work with her. I could not believe it. He gave in. I guess he got tired of the drive. I started to confide in the young lady I was riding to work with. She would pick me up in the morning and she could tell I was bothered or upset about something. I told her that I have got to leave him or else I was going to lose my mind. I tried to hold on to what faith I had left.

He had class on Monday nights so I was going to leave him then. I had already told my oldest daughter to start packing because we were going to hide our bags. The young lady and her husband were going to assist me. They came over while he was in class and threw our things in the car. I got money out of the bank and we were gone. I felt free finally. I did not care anymore. I could finally be the person I was before I met him.

I knew once he got home from class he would realize we were gone and know where we were and would call. He did just that. He called my mother's house. I answered the phone. He was apologetic for how he treated us and asked me to come back. Not to take his children from him. He promised he would change which he had never said before and that let me know he knew what he was doing was wrong. I let him get to me. I wanted to be true to my wedding vows after all I was a pastor's wife and the vows said for better or for worse. I started to feel bad but I did not trust him. I believed he would still act the same. He said he would be there to pick us up in the morning. I told him no. I was not leaving and that he could call back later. I did not know what to do. Should I stay or should I go. I needed time to think.

That was the best rest I had in a long time. I slept like a baby. I honestly did not miss him. I felt renewed. I knew I could make it without him. I was a strong woman but I had allowed him to break me, to control my every move. How could I have allowed such a thing? I am a faithful wife but not his doormat. Lord, what is your plan for me in this marriage? I needed answers I didn't know. My heart said not to go back but I am being lead to return, why? I do remember him telling me before that if I ever left him he would find me and harm everyone and my mother. I never mentioned that to anyone. Was he serious? Did I want to take that chance to find out? He was very calm on the phone when we spoke so in the back of my mind I wondered if he had a motive.

I decided to go back so I told him to come pick us up. My oldest daughter was very upset. I just thought she is a child and doesn't understand. I made a vow to God and I trusted Him to bring me through. God created him and He has everything in control.

When I returned home I found out I was 3 months pregnant. I never told anyone in the church that I had actually left him.

Things were going well in the church. I loved my church family and I knew they loved me and the children; however, I knew they had their reservations about my husband, their pastor, because of the control he had on his family. There was a family in the church that was really close to my oldest daughter and wanted to take her under their wing. He wouldn't allow her to spend much time with them. He had to control everything.

I was 9 months pregnant at this time with our third child. The church had an appreciation service for me on a Saturday. My mother and aunt came to the service to support me. As I was sitting in the service I went into labor and had to leave the service. I was told the service was awesome. I gave birth to my third daughter. I remember him saying she was not as pretty as our first child we had together. I looked at him like he was crazy because he was always saying something stupid out of his mouth.

We needed someone to watch our youngest daughter she was 3 years old at the time. There was this young lady at our church who I had gotten to know and I befriended her. I wanted to help her out because I knew she did not have a job and she could help me out by watching our daughter. She had just moved in her apartment and we helped her out financially by getting some utilities turned on for her. We talked to her about the possibility of watching our daughter during the day at our house. She agreed to it.

During this time she began to confide in my husband about certain things which was understandable because he was the pastor Apparently she allowed for her boyfriend to move into her place and my husband talked to her about her situation. I don't know what he would say exactly but I do remember him telling me this one particular time that she was upset with him. I asked him why and he said she did not like what he said to her. I did not ask about it anymore I just let it go.

CHAPTER VIII

About a week later one of the members from our church who had become a very good friend had come to our house that evening. The expression on her face was one of great concern and hurt. I could tell it was difficult for her to even begin the conversation. I got butterflies in my stomach just watching her. What in the world was going on? Why was she so upset? She finally started to talk. She started off by saying she doesn't really know what to say because it was difficult for her. Then she said the person that had been babysitting for us called her and confided in her about something. She came out and said it. She said the young lady told her that she had been sleeping with my husband, her pastor. My heart dropped. I could not believe what I was hearing. This man is a husband, father, a pastor, a man of God. Even though our marriage was not perfect, I know he loved God too much to cross that line at least. She said she was going to the Deacons of the church to tell them about the situation. I felt violated on so many levels. I trusted her with my child, I trusted her in my home, and helped her financially. Then I was angry with my husband because how could he have let himself even get in that situation whether it is true or not true.

He finally spoke and asked our friend if she was serious about what she had just said. She replied that she was serious. He said he could not believe it. We both advised him that he should go to the Deacons before she did so it wouldn't appear as if he was trying to hide anything. I supported him because I did not believe or want to believe that he would do something like that. So begin that faithful wife that I was, once again I had his back.

He spoke with the Deacons to tell them something important had come up and he needed to meet with them. We met with them and they assured him that he did not have anything to worry about and she had not come to them about anything and to wait and see what happens.

Well it happened. It got out. Everybody in the church was talking about it. The church had become divided. There were those who believed it happened and those that did not believe it happened. It was a mess. People were not speaking to each other including me. I would go to church and only speak to those that I knew were on my husband's side. I know God was not pleased with this behavior. He was not pleased with his people. We were just going through the motions of fellowship, church service, praising God. It was horrible. It had gotten to the point where those that believed the rumors did not want him to continue as pastor. They wanted to bring it before the church and vote on whether he was to continue as pastor.

A church meeting was called. I believe every member showed up even those who did not attend church often. The purpose of the meeting was to determine, based on the accusations, if the congregation wanted him to continue to serve as pastor. This was very difficult for me. We sat beside each other during the meeting and one by one different people started standing up giving details about what they had heard. In my opinion the meeting had turned into an I heard this, well I heard that kind of meeting. Yes, I was very embarrassed to sit there and hear all the things that were being said. People were angry, those who believed the rumors and those who did not believe the rumors. I could understand the anger, confusion, and resentment. I was torn as well but I could not tell anyone how I felt about the whole situation. So I appeared to be the supportive wife. I was angry because I felt betrayed by the woman who started all the confusion as well as my husband for putting himself in this situation. I am carrying this man's baby and people in this meeting are giving details about what allegedly happened between him and this woman. It was almost like they were mad at me for being married to him and staying with him after all this mess came out. They did not know my own personal hell I was going through mentally and emotionally.

Well, the Deacons finally put an end to all of the open discussion and asked that the congregation vote. "Everyone in favor of the pastor keeping his position raise your hand" every hand went up, everyone in favor of relieving him from the duty as pastor show by raising your hand. Not a single hand went up. I was amazed. There was a deacon that my husband was close to and he told him that he would have had more confidence in him if he had come out and said those things never happened. That has always been an issue for me; he never denied the allegations openly.

There was still tension at the church for awhile. We had even found out she had started saying she was pregnant by him; seems like things had gone from bad to worse. What in the world? God, how am I going to keep the faith, it seems like once I get through one wave another one is right there to take me out. How could this be happening? Through this entire ordeal, my husband never spoke up for himself. I would tell him that he needed to openly defend himself but he never would so of course even though I supported him openly I started to have my doubts.

We got the news that she had lost the baby and that she was going to have a funeral service. Myself along with some members of the church that I was close to, counted the months and according to our calculation he could not have been the father of her baby. The bottom line is no one really knows if anything ever happened between them, but God and them.

After we went through that ordeal at the church things were never the same. So much had been said and done. I am sure the members still had their doubts even the ones that supported him I did as well because he never denied anything.

He felt the tension at church so he thought it would be a good idea to leave and start his own ministry, he did just that. Our family was still growing. I was now pregnant with our fourth and as far as I was concerned final child. A few members left with us and some from other ministries joined the new church as well. We were able to get a building and with donations from other ministries we were able to get the work done to the building that needed to be done. Once again I thought this new ministry would improve things in our home. I thought I would be able to have adult relationships outside my home other than him. I thought I would be able to at least go out to dinner or shopping with women in the church. Well that did not happen. I just could not figure him out. He was insane.

I use to sing and direct the choir when I was younger. I never told him that but he made me the praise and worship leader at the new ministry. That helped to bring me out of the shell I had developed while I was married to him. When we would have guest ministers at our church they would come up to me after service and compliment me on the praise and worship. I could not believe he would get jealous about that. He wanted to know what they said and he did not want me to hug them or look at them when I would talk to them. He even started accusing me of being attracted to men in the church. I finally told him that he was the one with the self esteem issues and that I refuse to allow him to put that on me and maybe he should have married an unattractive woman with self esteem issues if he was that concerned about other men. I also told him that I made my vows before God and I took them seriously and I had never thought about other men. Now that I think about it, was he accusing me because of what he was doing?

He was a full time pastor at his new ministry and he now had a job with the school system at the alternative school working with at risk students. He also worked part time as a mentor for youth and with mentally challenged adults. I gave birth to our son and we agreed that I return to work. I wanted to work in education. I was able to get a job as a teacher assistant. I loved my new job. It would appear that life was good. Our children were healthy; we really did not have money issues because we were both working. Had he changed? No!

We had one car so he would take me to work and drop me off. Our schools were walking distance from each other. I had been working at the school for about one month.

CHAPTER IX

It was October 2001. I will never forget this month and year because my life changed forever.

We had just gotten home from work. I was getting the children situated and I heard a knock at the door. He got to the door before I did, so I continued. He opened the door and I heard a male voice, he asked for my oldest daughter. He said her first and last name. I immediately became concerned. My husband asked if there was something he could help the gentleman with. He replied no, I want to speak to and he said her name again. At this time I walked to the door to see what was going on. My husband left from the door to go get my daughter. I noticed a man and woman standing at the door waiting for my daughter. At this time I introduced myself to them and they introduced themselves to me. The woman told me her name and said she was from Child Protective Services and the man gave me his name and said he was a detective.

Child Protective Services and a detective at my house, what are they doing here? Has someone called them to my home? We don't abuse our children, so I thought. Lord you are my strength I trust you will prepare me for what I am about to go through and by faith I will be able to share the story of my "Life After Silent Tears".

They asked me and my daughter to step outside so they could talk to us. Immediately I felt faint and weak. *What in the world is going on? Why are they at my home asking to speak to my baby?* They asked me and my daughter to take a ride with them to their office. I did not even go back into the house to let my husband know. I don't even think I took my purse. We got in the back seat of the car. That was the longest ride of my life. I looked at my daughter and whispered to her, do you know what is going on? She looked at me with this blank look on her face. From the look on her face, I knew something horrible had happened.

We arrived to their office. They had me wait in this lounge area while they took her to the back. I asked if I could go with her and they assured me they would be with me soon. It seemed as though I waited in that room for hours. I was extremely nervous. Everything was going through my mind. I could not imagine why we were even there. *What were they talking to my daughter about? I had not done anything wrong. Had someone called them and lied on us?* I paced back and forth, I sat down, I stood up, I prayed. What was taking them so long? What are they saying to my child? What are they asking her? Is she scared? She needs me!

Finally, they came to get me. I followed them to their office. My daughter was sitting on the couch so I sat beside her. The social worker and the detective sat across from us. The social worker says to me "your daughter has something to tell you". I look at my baby, she start to cry. I immediately hugged her. I felt in my heart what she was about to tell me.

My daughter could not speak because she was crying very hard and I was holding her tightly. I could tell she was extremely hurt about something. I looked at the social worker and said "can someone please tell me what is going on"? I was starting to feel sick. I was concerned about my other babies. The social worker said your daughter confided in a friend today at school and the friend talked to a guidance counselor. Then she continued, your husband has touched your daughter inappropriately.

At that moment my mind, body, spirit, and soul went completely numb. Did I hear her correctly? This man who I married, who has been part of our lives since she was 7 years old and now she is 14 has hurt my baby like this! I sat there hugging my daughter and we both cried. All I could say was "oh my God, I am so sorry", and I asked her why didn't she tell me. She said she was scared.

Once I got my self together I asked them if they were going to take my children from me. They told me no because they know I had no idea he had done this. Then I said my kids are with him now and I have to get them. I asked what was going to happen now. The detective stated he was going to get a couple of state troopers to go to the house to arrest him.

This did not seem real. I am the wife of a pastor, a mother, an educated woman. This man may have been abusive to me but to have violated an innocent child, a child that considered him to be her father. How dare he!

At that moment having the love of Christ went out the window. I wanted to take matters into my own hands. I wanted to hurt him because he hurt my baby. I was not going to have mercy on him. The only thing that bought me back to reality was the fact that I have to take care of these children. If something was to happen to me who was going to care for my babies. I needed to get my other children away from him. My world as I knew it had come crashing down.

How was I going to get the kids from him without letting him know what was going on? They told me to call to see if he was at the house and they would wait till we were out the house to arrest him. I called the house and he did not answer the phone. Where could he have gone and why would he leave the house? It came to me to call my son's godmother. I called her and she told me that he had dropped the kids off with her. I asked her what did he say to her. She said he just asked her to watch the kids for awhile. I told her I would be there later to pick them up.

That was so strange to me. Why would you drop the children off? Did he know what was going on? I informed the social worker and the detective that the children were not at the house so the detective made the call to the police department.

There was a business across the street from the house. I told the social worker to park there because my daughter and I did not want to be there when they arrest him. The van was in the driveway so he had returned home. As we sat there my mind was blank. Everything was happening so fast. My family was about to be split. I was about to become a single mother of 4 children ages 14, 5, 2, 1. He use to tell me that I would not be able to make it without him. He would also say no one would want me with 4 children. Was what he told me true? He had broken my will to the point where I believed those words.

CHAPTER X

The detective and state troopers pull up. They knocked on the door. He opened the door and they went into the house. I started to become emotional. I could not believe they were about to arrest my husband, who was a pastor, a mentor, a father. The door opened and they brought him out of the house in handcuffs. My daughter and I both broke down and started crying. It was hard for both of us to see this. Even though we knew he had hurt her, it was hard seeing that because he was the father of my children. I will never get that vision out of my mind.

My life as I knew it changed. Now, I know that my life was not the best before all of this, but I guess it was the comfort of knowing my children had a mother and a father in the home and the comfort of knowing he was a hard worker who made sure the bills were paid. The reality was he was not who he represented himself to be and I was miserable and now he had done the unspeakable. I needed God to help me because I never dreamed I would have to face this or be put in a situation of this magnitude.

After they took him away, the social worker took me to get my other babies. The godmother could tell something was wrong. She asked me what was going on. All I said was I would talk to her later. When I returned home the detective was still there. He wanted to get some items out of the house for evidence. This was like something you would see in a movie. I was walking through the house in tears. I felt as though I was going to lose my mind. This was too much.

I needed my mother. I called her and explained to her what was going on and she came to us that same night. I could not sleep that night. I could not get this situation out of my mind. I know my daughter felt like it was all her fault but I reassured her it was not and that she had done nothing wrong.

I am now responsible for these 4 children. I have to pay a mortgage, car payment, and take care of all the household bills by myself. Thinking about everything that had transpired in my life within that 24 hour period, I felt myself becoming faint in my faith.

I felt God had forsaken me because he had allowed this to happen to my daughter. Everyone was going to find out about what had happened in my family and we were very private people. I never shared what I was going through with anyone. Now he had been exposed! I did not even want to compare this with the saying "what the devil meant for evil God used it for my good". How could this be used for my good? I have been betrayed. I could take all the abuse but as a mother I always wanted to protect my children from any harm. That was my worse fear and it had come to pass.

The next day was his bond hearing. Yes, I went. I wanted to look in his face. I needed to talk to him so he could tell me that this was all a mistake or explain to me why he had done this, of course there was no explanation for that and I just wanted to reach out and touch him, literally. They bought him into the courtroom with handcuffs and shackles. This strong, controlling, mean, abusive, arrogant man now looked humbled, weak, scared, and broken. He looked the way I felt for so many years being married to him. He made eye contact with me and never said a word.

The bond was set and I knew he was not going to get out. I left the courtroom went home and broke down. I felt like I was going to snap. I felt helpless. I could not face anyone so I stopped going to work. I was not making enough to pay the mortgage or car payment anyway. The van was repossessed because I did not make the payment but it was in his name so I did not care. My mother bought me a car and put it in my name which was a blessing. I did not even think about how I was going to survive. I felt like giving up. Everyone knew what had happened to my family. It was on the local news that evening and on the front page of the paper.

My mother was very supportive. For about a month she would stay with us off and on. She would prepare dinner and do as much as she could to give me a break. There was a special pastor and his wife that were there for me and my family during this time. They made sure we had plenty of food to eat and even blessed us financially.

About 2 months after he was arrested I was able to get in touch with my best friend of about 12 years. We had lost contact for many years and it was literally a miracle that I was able to get the number of a mutual friend who was able to put me in contact with her.

I will never forget this moment. I called her and asked to speak to her, she immediately recognized my voice and she started to cry. I will always cherish that moment. I began to tell her about what has recently transpired in my life and she suggested that I come for a visit. Lord knows that was just what I needed. I needed to get away from everything. I told my mother about wanting to go visit her and she was very supportive and agreed that I should go and she agreed to watch the children for me.

The moment that I made the decision to go visit my best friend, it is hard to explain but I felt as though weights had been lifted. I felt as if I was free. My mind had become clear. I felt like I was becoming the person I use to be before I had married him. I felt as though I had approval from God to go on with my life and the confidence and assurance in him that he was going to make a way for me and my children. It was like he took every worry, guilt, and burden from me. It was like God was telling me this is my new beginning.

Chapter XI

The weekend had arrived for me to go visit my best friend. I arrived to her home and she met me outside. We hugged then she looked at me. She was always honest with me in the past and I loved her for that. She said you don't look like the person I use to know. You are not fly like you were in college. You are not the person I use to know. I said yeah I know, girl I have been through so much these past years.

It was like time had stood still for us. We reminisced about all the fun times we had in the past and my current situation. We were sorry we had lost touch but grateful we had reconnected. I needed that visit and little did I know this was going to be the beginning of a new life for me and my family.

She talked to me about the possibility of moving back to the area. I seriously considered that because I wanted to leave the past behind. I lived in the area before when I went to college. The idea seemed very refreshing because I knew I needed a fresh start. I had explained to her my concerns about needing to get a place and not getting approved because I did not have a job. She told me that the apartment manager where she lived was an older woman and that she believed that if I explained my situation to her she would be willing to give me an apartment. She said all utilities would be included in the rent and the complex had their own Section 8. I did not know what that was so she had to explain to me that Section 8 was a program that provided assistance with rent. Then I expressed my concern about still needing money for food and other minor expenses. She told me about how I could get assistance from social services and that I could also get assistance for child care. I was an educated woman with a Bachelors' degree. I did not need handouts but I was humbled and knew I had to start somewhere, I believed that God had a plan for me and my children. Therefore, I was willing to look into it if it meant this would be a way for me to move to the area and start a new life for me and my children.

The weekend had come to an end and I had made plans to come back the following weekend and stay till that Monday so that I could talk to the apartment complex manager. I returned home and talked to my oldest daughter and mother about what I wanted to do. They agreed it was a great idea to get away from all the drama.

I was keeping in touch with the Assistant District Attorney that was prosecuting the case and she informed me that they were going to offer him a plea bargain of 15 years but that if he did not accept the plea and we went to trial my daughter would have to testify and if he was found guilty he would be facing 20 years to life.

I returned back to visit my best friend the next weekend. I told her that I had decided it would be in the best interest of my family to leave the area and relocate. She was very happy and assured me she would do everything to help me. I was not nervous about my decision. I had a peace about it because I felt confident in God. During this time in my life, I would listen to Fred Hammond. His music got me through this test and toughest time in my life. He is my favorite gospel artist and hopefully one day I will meet him and share with him how his music ministered to me when I could not attend church because it reminded me of my husband and I needed time to get past that. His music helped me stay connected to God.

That Monday I went to speak to the property manager. I was nervous because I did not know what to expect. I am going to ask this woman to give me and my children a place to stay and I had no income. Talk about having faith. I did it, I went into the office. I began to tell her my situation and while talking to her I began to cry. I didn't want that to happen but of course I was still very emotional about what had happened in my life.

She empathized with me and gave me an apartment. The deposit was $99 and my rent was going to be $100 per month because she set me up with the Section 8 program. I was so grateful. I told my best friend and I immediately called my mother to tell her the great news. My mother gave me the money for the deposit. I was to move in March 1, 2002. That lease meant more to me than just having an apartment. It was a new beginning, a new "lease" on life.

I returned home and started making preparation to move. The only thing I took were our clothes and a few toys. I left everything else in that house. I could not get away fast enough. I did not even tell the Assistant

District Attorney that I was leaving the area. I wanted to get my children away from everything.

We moved into our new apartment. I did not have any furniture at the time and I did not even care. The feeling of freedom was very overwhelming; all I could do was cry. I thought about how God was just so awesome. No, I did not have a job but at this point I had a place for my children to live and a car to drive. It was just a matter of time before I would get a job because this was only the beginning.

CHAPTER XII

The next day my best friend took me to social services to apply for assistance. I got approved for the assistance so I was able to get food and pay my rent; yes another blessing. No, I had never been on assistance before but I knew it was God's method to my madness. He was beginning his restoration process in my life. I registered my two oldest for school the following day and I was home with the youngest two and I began my job search.

I was still broken spiritually. I did not want to visit any churches. I could not even watch ministries on television because a sermon may be preached that reminded me of my husband. I had faith in God because I knew he was with me in the midst of my storm but my trust in "the church" had diminished drastically. I knew I could not put all preachers in the same category but I was having my spiritual, emotional, and mental struggles.

The next month after we moved to the area God blessed me with a job. I was employed with a telecommunication company. Through a program with social services I was able to work and continue to get assistance which was a tremendous help.

Remember I said we moved and I did not tell the Assistant District attorney where I was? Well one day there was a knock at my door. I opened it and this young lady introduced herself and said she was from (CPS) Child Protective Services). Oh no, not again! I immediately got an attitude. I asked her what she was doing here and what did she want. She asked if she could come in.

Once she came inside she made me feel a little more at ease. She said my previous state had contacted her department and explained the situation and wanted her to set up counseling for us. I stopped feeling defensive once she explained that to me. I listened to her and was receptive to what she was saying. I would imagine they found out where I was living because of the assistance I was receiving from social services.

I never thought about getting counseling but God knew that was what we needed so he made it happen by allowing them to find us. By doing this, God was continuing the healing process in our lives. Not only was he meeting our financial needs, he was meeting our emotional needs.

During this time, I had filed for divorce. I needed closure so that I could become whole and move on with my life. He signed the papers and I was free. Also during this time I was contacted by the Assistant District Attorney. She told me that he had accepted the plea bargain for 15 years and that my daughter did not have to return to testify. We were relieved. I felt that if he was innocent he would go to trial to fight for his life so by him taking the plea his actions spoke volumes.

I wanted to get back in education but did not know where to begin. The job at the telecommunication company was ok but I wanted more. I asked my best friend if she could tell me where the school board office was. She did and on my day off I went there to put in an application to be a teacher's assistant for summer school.

The receptionist at the human resource office for the school district was very helpful to me. I completed the application. She told me that all the summer school positions were filled but that there was still a need for an assistant teacher in the ESL (English Second Language) class. This class would consist of students from other countries that needed to learn how to speak English. I told her I was very interested in the position and I was able to interview with the Director of that department that very same day and was hired. Once again, God was reassuring me that he had my back.

I resigned from the telecommunication company and began working as a teacher assistant with the ESL students. The school was walking distance from where I lived. I enjoyed working with the teacher and the students. They were eager to learn. I realized that I wanted to work as a teacher assist for the regular school year. I had to apply for that position as well which I did.

Before summer school was over, I received a call from an elementary school principal who wanted to schedule an interview. I was very excited and happy that I received a call for an interview. I went to the interview and the next day I received a call from the assistant principal offering me the job as a kindergarten teacher assistant.

Of course I accepted the offer. God's blessing were flowing and overtaking me. We did not have a need or a want for anything. My desire was to return to school to obtain my Masters Degree in Education with a concentration in school counseling which would increase my pay and allow for me to get off the system and be able to be completely self sufficient. I would be able to provide for my children and purchase a home for them.

School started in the fall and I had a great working relationship with the teacher to whom I was an assistant. I loved my job, but I wanted more. This position was just a stepping stone.

On this particular day I went to pick my son up from day care and I picked up a copy of a Parent Magazine. On the back of the magazine there was an advertisement for Continuing Education at a school called Cambridge College. What caught my attention were the days the classes were offered which were weekends and they offered the area of study I wanted which was school counseling.

When I was married I always wanted to return to college but my husband was never supportive. He was insecure about my interest and the advancements I wanted to make in life.

I applied to the college and was accepted. I was now going to college full time on the weekends, working full time during the week and a full time mother. My children were my motivation and my oldest was a big help to me.

The second year of my employment with the school district the school I worked for was going to close. All the faculty and staff were assigned to other schools. By this time I had completed all of my coursework for my Masters. The only thing left for me to do was complete my internship. I wanted to be able to work on my internship full time so I was torn between going to my new assigned school, resigning from my current position and completing my internship which was non-paid and a total of 720 hours which averaged to about a 4 month process.

I had to step out on faith so I decided to resign and work to on my internship full time. I submitted my paperwork to the college and the school district which I worked for approval for me to complete these hours through their schools, I was approved.

CHAPTER XIII

So now I did not have a job at this point but I was still receiving financial assistance from social services. I was told by them that in order to continue receiving assistance I would have to work at least 20 hours per week. I became discouraged, how was I going to do that if I was working on my internship hours full-time. That was going to be my full time non-compensated employment for the next 4 months. When was I going to be able to work 20 hours. I began brainstorming and it came to me. I could go through a temporary agency and work on the weekends.

I contacted a temporary agency that I had heard great things about. I took their test, completed the necessary paperwork and they hired me to work for them. Now, watch God. They contacted me within that same week for an assignment that was for weekends. I interviewed with the manager and she hired me. It was a temporary assignment for as long as I wanted the job and it was for a company that sold homes to retired couples and I was the receptionist.

I loved the job. There were 4 realtors in the office. They knew my schedule and that I was completing my graduate school assignment. They were very supportive and encouraging. It was as if God had handpicked this temporary place of employment for me.

My internship had come to an end and a good friend of mine that I met in graduate school contacted me in reference to a job for a well known Telecommunication Company. The company had great pay which was weekly and excellent benefits. It was not in the education field but I knew this would be a way for me to completely get off the system and that was my ultimate goal. I had completed my internship and was preparing for graduation. I graduated in May 2007. As long as I had my master's degree

I knew I would still have the opportunity to get back into education. I needed the money right now because I wanted to make some moves.

My friend gave me the contact information for the human resource person that was setting up testing for the company. I called and she set up the testing. I passed the test and then an interview was scheduled. I had the interview about a week after I completed the test and about 2 weeks after the interview I received a call with a job offer and I accepted it. Ok God, now we are full speed ahead.

My children were doing well in school. They were honor roll students and had perfect attendance. I was not receiving any child support. All of our needs were being met. And to think, my ex-husband told me that I would not be able to make it without him.

In March 2007, I started my training at my new job. The job was about a 45 minute commute each way. I finished my training successfully in about 2 months and graduated from graduate school in May 2007. My mother and children attended my graduation. I wanted that to be a message to them that we must put God first and there isn't anything we can't do. God allowed me to be able to get off the system. I loved my job because of the provision it made for my children.

My goal was to purchase a house so we started looking. I found a house and my children and I would ride by it to look at it and check out the neighborhood. We agreed that I should purchase it. In January 2008 I was able to purchase a home for my family. Once again I remembered the words of my ex-husband; I would never be able to make it on my own. Now I realized he was right. I made it with God.

I had never owned a brand new car before. In April 2008 I purchased my first brand new car. Now it was starting to make sense, God was giving me "Double for my Trouble". He provided a means of escape for me and my children even though His method of escape was devastating. He knew the big picture. He gave my daughter the strength she needed to tell someone so she could be safe and she did not want what happened to her to happen to her siblings.

He knew that if I had tried to leave and divorce my ex-husband under normal circumstances I would have never had any peace. I would be fighting for custody of my children. He would have tried to control every aspect of my life. My life would be full of constant drama.

I know this to be true because of the fact he took me to court for visitation. I did not even want the children to know that their father was incarcerated. I wanted to protect them from that information. By him doing that, that showed me that he still wanted to have control. We went to court. They bought him in handcuffed and shackled. I had not seen him in about 6 years. He was sitting off to the side. I looked at him, he looked at me and he mouthed "please forgive me". Before I knew it I said "I already have". I know that was a breaking point and a release for me.

Yes, this horrible thing happened to me and my family but God was there with us throughout the process. He did not let me fail. He gave me the strength that I did not think I had to endure.

Things had started to change at my job. The company became less flexible and they started to extend the hours and wanted us to start working on Saturdays. I know it was time to move on. I wanted to get back into education as a school counselor.

I found out about a youth residential treatment facility that was hiring in the educational department. I contacted them and completed the application. I was contacted for an interview. I was interviewed by the assistant principal. She informed me that they had an opening for an English teacher. The interview went well. I was told what the starting salary would be and in order to be eligible for a salary increase I needed to complete a Laws and Regulation class in special education.

I received a call a few days later with a job offer. I started to panic. I wanted to leave my current employer but all I kept thinking about was the pay cut and the fact that I just bought a home and a car and how was I going to afford to transition from my current job to this new job. I did not accept the job.

I took what the assistant principal had said about needing to complete that one class so that my pay would increase seriously because I really wanted to work for that company. I immediately enrolled in school again and my job paid for my classes. I returned to the same graduate school. This time I was taking classes in special education. I completed the Law and Regulation Class for special education about 5 months later.

I called the youth residential treatment facility to see if there were currently any positions available. Now the assistant principal was the Director of Education and she informed me that I needed to complete another application and she would schedule another interview.

My current job was not enjoyable anymore. We were micromanaged and you always had to look over your shoulder and watch your back. I knew I had to step out on faith because it had gotten to the point where you did not know if you had a job from day to day.

I scheduled another interview with the Director of Education at the youth residential facility. Human resources called me about a week later with another job offer as an English teacher and this time I accepted. I was still uncomfortable about the salary but I knew God had not brought me this far to leave me.

While I was in the position of English teacher the Director of Education knew I had my Masters in school counseling so we discussed the possibility of creating a school counseling position for me and I would also be an assistant to her.

About 6 months after I had started working as a English teacher my director was able to get the position of school counselor approved. I was now the school counselor for the education department for the youth residential treatment facility and an assistant to the Director of Education.

CHAPTER XIV

God had started me from humble beginnings. He took me through stages in my life to get me to the place I am today. He has his hands on my children and through it all they are whole and wonderful children. They are active in church and they have healthy relationships with other children. Even though there was a void in their life because of the absence of their father, God has given them normal lives.

My oldest has a very productive life. She has certifications in nursing and is a wonderful mother. She is raising a smart, healthy, witty son.

Throughout my refining process, I still had bumps and hurdles but God put the people I needed in my life to get me through. My children's godmother kept inviting me to visit her church. I did visit for about 2 years and finally I decided to join. My youngest two are youth ushers and my youngest daughter is a member of the praise dance ministry. My son is in the TAG (Talent and Gifted) program at school. He is a comedian and he loves to play football which is a natural ability. He is a great football player for his age. My second oldest daughter loves photography and she loves to draw and write. She is very artistic.

I am grateful to God for all he has done and going to continue to do in my life. I graduated with my second masters in June 2010. I am currently enrolled in a Doctorate program. If everything goes well I should have my Doctorate degree in Educational Leadership and Management in 2012.

As you reflect on the introduction remember we must forgive. Is that an easy thing to do? No, it is not. Did I struggle with hatred and wished harm would come to my ex-husband? Yes I did. Was it easy to forgive? No it was not. Did it make me a stronger person? Yes it did. If I held on to all the hurt and allow hate to control me then I would not be in the place I am in my life. I refused to continue being the victim and now through Christ I am the victor. I am thankful for my "Life After Silent Tears". To God Be the Glory!

Lightning Source UK Ltd.
Milton Keynes UK
UKOW04f0111200917
309503UK00001B/119/P